PRAISE ABOUT THE AUTHORS

"Cybersecurity has always been about staying ahead of the bad guy, but what if that were impossible? What would you do? We must all adopt a holistic mindset of cybersecurity, and Jim and John's book helps readers to understand the risk they face and how to think beyond 'staying ahead.'"

Stuart McClure

CEO at Cylance, Inc.

"*Wolves, Sheep, and Sheepdogs* is filled with timeless principles which helps me navigate the disorienting storm of cybersecurity risk and the endless tidal waves of over-promised, under-delivered solutions. The brilliance of *Wolves, Sheep, and Sheepdogs* is its ability to articulate these timeless truths through clever analogies and simple language, providing a common reference from which C-level executives, highly technical staff, and key stakeholders can communicate as an orchestrated, harmonious team."

Dean Sheley

CISO for South Dakota South Dakota Board of Regents

"We engaged the services of Jim Shaeffer, along with JCS & Associates, Inc., to help us deploy a security solution that better protects against the advanced threats that are prevalent today. Jim and his technical team were very helpful and did a great job getting everything installed and configured correctly."

Lowell Goemaat

Network Administrator at Harbor Group/Interstates

"Working with JCS & Associates, Inc., and Jim Shaeffer in particular, has allowed us to deploy a security solution that helps me sleep better at night. Jim and his technical team go above and beyond what others in his industry do to make sure we are a happy customer."

Dan Marini

Senior Network Administrator at Quincy Credit Union

"I recently worked with Jim Shaeffer from JCS & Associates, Inc. to test, purchase, and deploy a next-generation antivirus solution. Previously, this solution had been unavailable for a customer of our size (<250) for purchase, let alone as a proof of concept. Jim worked with us and the vendor to make it happen and treated us with the attention normally afforded much larger organizations! We definitely appreciated this level of attention and were able to implement that next-generation antivirus solution in a very short amount of time. I look forward to working with JCS & Associates, Inc. more in the future!"

Clint Woodrow

System Administrator/Tech Lead at Oregon Department of State Lands

"JCS & Associates, Inc. helped us procure and implement our new endpoint security application here at Concordance Healthcare Solutions. We couldn't be more satisfied with the outcome. Jim and his staff are friendly, knowledgeable, and always eager to help."

Eric Rise

Network Administrator at Concordance Healthcare Solutions

"I have had the privilege of partnering with JCS & Associates, Inc. on numerous occasions to help solve security challenges. Jim Shaeffer and his staff have always been great to work with. They take the time to understand our needs and work with us to identify the most effective solution for our business."

Chuck Cinco

Director of Information Security, Premier Bankcard LLC

WOLVES, SHEEP, AND SHEEPDOGS

A LEADER'S GUIDE TO INFORMATION SECURITY

JIM SHAEFFER AND JOHN PAUL CUNNINGHAM

WOLVES, SHEEP, AND SHEEPDOGS

A LEADER'S GUIDE TO INFORMATION SECURITY

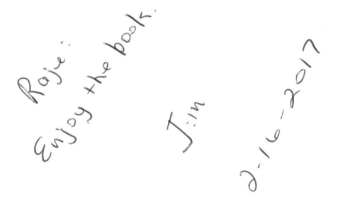

JIM SHAEFFER AND JOHN PAUL CUNNINGHAM

THRONE
PUBLISHING GROUP

Throne Publishing Group
2329 N Career Ave #215
Sioux Falls, SD 57107
ThronePG.com

TABLE OF CONTENTS

TABLE OF CONTENTS

INTRODUCTION

In the information security world, threats grow more sophisticated by the day. Whether they are impersonation emails or brute-force attacks, new threats require a fresh outlook. In this book, you will find profiles of major security threats as well as a picture of how the best chief information security officers (CISOs) think and respond to such threats. Our goal is to offer insight, strategies, and tactics to help you become what we call an adaptive organization. Adaptive organizations are the ones whose breaches never make the headlines because they stop security incidents dead in their tracks. They are the organizations that don't simply keep ahead of the curve: they define it.

We have worked with hundreds of organizations of varying security postures and risk appetites. However, the common denominator that distinguishes great organizations from all others is the presence of a great "sheepdog"—a leader who can create an adaptive security posture capable of broad organizational engagement and who can rapidly counter and respond to any threat. As you will see, we have written this book using a helpful analogy, "The Pasture," whose main characters are the shepherd, the sheepdog, the sheep, and the wolves. By doing so, we hope to create a common language for those in information security and those in the non-technical C-suite. We believe this is critical because protecting an organization's most valuable assets should be everyone's concern.

Additionally, our perspectives combine to provide a well-rounded outline of the *what*, *why*, and *how* of cybersecurity today. Every chapter includes insight from both of us, Jim and John, to give you a full picture of the best principles and methods you can employ. Thus, whether you are a CEO, a CISO, or anyone in between, read this book with a reflective eye so you can evaluate your security position today and chart a course to strengthening it tomorrow. Now, let's turn to the story of a shepherd and his sheepdog and see what they have to teach us about cybersecurity in today's wolf-ridden landscape.

PART ONE

FORTIFY

CHAPTER 1

THE SHEEPDOG

The cybersecurity world is a whirlwind of change and ever-evolving opportunities and threats. I have seen virus after virus repackaged and deployed. I have cleaned up countless environments and consulted on prevention and infrastructure. What I have discovered is that more important than any one skillset is a mindset that includes the ability to be adaptive, vigilant, and constantly aware of potential threats. That's why John and I wrote this book. It's a leader's guide to navigating the information security world with minimal loss of assets. John is an experienced CISO and brings a wealth of wisdom from decades of work inside organizations of every size.

As a consultative salesperson, I have worked with John for many years. As our relationship has grown, so has our understanding of what it takes to protect data from both external and internal threats. We can best sum up the knowledge and strategies we would like to share with you in an analogy that most would never associate with the security world: the analogy of "The Pasture".

We have found that this analogy paints a vivid picture of the principle workings every organization faces, and it provides a common language for both technically skilled professionals and nontechnical

"We've written this book because data asset protection has never been more vital to companies, and it will only continue to increase."

business leaders. We've written this book because data asset protection has never been more vital to companies, and it will only continue to increase. Therefore, we will share the story of the pasture and ask you to follow our guide to effective cybersecurity and adopt the mindsets required to stay ahead of the wolves who are constantly trying to steal your sheep.

THE ANALOGY OF THE PASTURE

Imagine a flock of sheep grazing in a pasture. They bleat back and forth, munching easily on the grass. The forested hill country that surrounds them is bathed in sunlight, and the sheep don't have a care in the world. Their shepherd moves from one to the other, looks them over, and pats their thick wool coats. He tends them as he would on any other day. They are his livelihood.

An old wooden fence marks a sturdy perimeter around his field. It's been there for years, as long as the shepherd can remember. He's only ever had to make light repairs to it. So to him, it's always done its job. But as the sheep mill about him, he hears a sound distinct from their bleating: a low growl, rumbling just over the hilltop ahead. The shepherd squints and looks to the rocks that mark the top of the grassy knoll, then steps away from the flock and runs up the hill.

The growling intensifies as he climbs, so he runs faster. Then, cresting the top, he sees a tussle of fur and teeth. Two canines, one black and one brown, snarl and nip at one another. They circle one another, facing off with hackles up and teeth bared. The shepherd recognizes each animal immediately: a black wolf and the shepherd's vigilant brown sheepdog. The shepherd raises his tending hook and yells, "Get away, wolf! Get away!"

Both animals snap their heads in his direction. The wolf crouches lower, staring back and forth from the shepherd to the sheepdog. The sheepdog sees his shepherd, stands taller, and assumes an offensive posture. The shepherd runs, waving his staff wildly. With the sheepdog and his shepherd standing as a united front, the wolf realizes he has met his match and retreats. With a final snarl, he runs off toward the old wooden fence and easily leaps it without missing a stride. The shepherd watches the black wolf bound away.

"We haven't seen a wolf on our land in years," he says to the sheepdog. "It's a good thing you were here. Now, we'd better get back to the flock."

They amble back up the hill, the highest point on the shepherd's land. He stands on a moss-covered rock, surveying his wooden perimeter and flock. He counts his sheep and breathes a sigh of relief that they are all there.

Then he traces the fence line, looking for breaches to mend, but he sees none. *Not that it matters,* he says to himself. *The fence didn't stop that black wolf.*

But something still troubles him. Then he remembers that wolves are pack animals. They are masters of subterfuge and misdirection, and they rarely hunt alone. He looks intently at the upward-sloping land beyond his fence posts. Then, one by one, the shepherd sees four silent sentries watching every move he and his sheepdog make. On the side of an adjacent hill sit a red wolf, a gray wolf, a white wolf, and the black wolf they just chased off. It's chilling to see these predators so close, studying the shepherd, the sheepdog, and his flock.

After a few moments each wolf trots off, disappearing into the nearby tree line: first the red, then the gray and the white. However, the black remains for a moment, giving the shepherd and sheepdog a final glare. Then he follows the others into the woods. The shepherd stares at the trees and knows that the situation for his pasture and flock has changed. Things are not as simple as they used to be, and his fence feels eerily inadequate against the predators.

The shepherd and his sheepdog amble down the hill and rejoin the flock. The sheep are just as they left them, chewing and bleating happily, blissfully ignorant of the wolves that had threatened them. The shepherd realizes the sheep are still doing their job: eating and growing, gaining value with each passing day. But to keep them protected, he and the sheepdog have some work ahead of them. Meanwhile, as he ponders the situation, he notices the sheepdog bounding toward the fence, closely inspecting the perimeter, investigating the situation, and assessing the danger. "There may be wolves," the shepherd says aloud, "but that's why God made sheepdogs."

OF WOLVES AND SHEEPDOGS

We love this analogy because it applies to so many aspects and avenues of life. From the business world to society as a whole, these characters surface everywhere. But we see them most clearly in cybersecurity. The fundamental truth is that there always are wolves who will try to breach our fences and steal our sheep. That is why we have sheepdogs to protect the fold. So let's take a closer look at our players and discover what we can learn from them. Who are the sheep, wolves, shepherds and sheepdogs?

Sheep

In information security, the sheep are the assets that need protection. They represent the value our businesses hold and can be anything from personnel to intellectual property. But the primary challenge when discussing our personnel resources is that they are often unaware of the threats that surround them.

> **"The fundamental truth is that there always are wolves who will try to breach our fences and steal our sheep."**

They exist in what we call "condition white", a mindset that focuses on tasks rather than on remaining alert for possible threats. From a security standpoint, the sheep are generally an organization's non-IT employees.

But the sheep are the most important facet of any organization because of the tremendous value they generate. They go to work and help businesses thrive in exchange for fair pay, and they never seek to harm other sheep or their organization. In the business environment, the sheep must be cared for and protected so they can fulfill their primary role: producing. In reality, they represent the entire livelihood of both shepherd and sheepdog.

Wolves

Next, we have the wolves—predators to the sheep and foils to the sheepdogs. They are the bad guys who do nothing but take what isn't theirs. They are the hackers who try to steal our information and acquire wealth by exploiting the sheep. A variety of motives drives them, just as there are a variety of wolves. In fact, you'll notice in our analogy that we referenced red, gray, white, and black wolves—but we'll discuss their differences in further detail in chapter four. What's important now is to understand their common denominator: wolves are always scheming to take your valuable assets. Even more devious, they are found not only outside your defenses; they lurk inside as well.

The wolves are constantly probing, trying to find ways inside. Today, they are doing so at unprecedented levels. From engineering malware for attacking specific companies and individuals to elaborate social engineering, the wolves' tactics are constantly evolving. We see this in the advent of ransomware and targeted phishing schemes. But the bottom line is that wolves are players who will never act in the interests of anyone but themselves.

Shepherds

Now, let's step back inside the fence and consider the shepherd. In simple terms, shepherds bear the ultimate responsibility for their flocks' health and safety. They are the CEOs, board of directors and, to some extent, the shareholders and investors of any organization.

The shepherds are charged with their organizations' growth and stability. While we won't discuss the shepherd's role in cybersecurity at great length in this book, it is still a critical piece of the puzzle. In our analogy, what would have happened if the shepherd had been disengaged or unresponsive to his sheepdog's alerts? Disaster would have struck. As we will see through the rest of the chapters, shepherds must rely heavily on their sheepdogs to achieve success as defined in their organization's mission statement.

Sheepdogs

Last come the sheepdogs, that rare breed of cybersecurity warrior with a finely tuned risk posture. They are trained professionals who are cut from a different cloth and who reflect a particular mindset; they are constantly concerned with the flock's safety. They are the vigilant protectors who understand the risk-mitigating measures necessary to safeguard their organization's assets. They know the events to watch for and what data to pay attention to. The sheepdogs are alert at all times because they know there are wolves about. Their mindset is one of guarded optimism.

Everything the sheepdogs do is for the benefit of the sheep, which is why they never have their heads in the clouds. Sheep live their lives in condition white: unaware and unprepared. They look like easy victims, easy marks. Sheepdogs, on the other hand, always wear their seatbelt because they understand that not every situation is under their control. Others speed through red lights and end up in hit-and-runs, but sheepdogs live in "condition yellow," relaxed and alert. They are aware of their environment. They keep their heads up. They look around and use all of their senses. Sheepdogs move from condition yellow to "condition orange" when they identify a specific, potential threat. From there, the sheepdog can ascertain when the threat becomes real and elevate their awareness to "condition red." At that point they have drawn the mental line in the sand, and once the identified threat crosses that line, the sheepdog knows how to react. The final condition, known as "condition black," is that point at which the threat crosses the previously determined line. The sheepdog then blocks everything else out and focuses on the steps necessary to deal with the threat. While the sheep live in condition white, the sheepdogs always keep their eyes open and their ears to the ground. They don't live in a state of paranoia; instead, they remain relaxed and alert.

MY ROLE AS A SHEEPDOG

In my work and my life, I am a sheepdog. I see myself as a protector both inside and outside the workplace because I want to help people who are in bad situations—or better yet, prevent those situations altogether. Like any good sheepdog, my basis for this approach is that I care about the sheep, and I want to see valuable assets protected from the wolves. That caring is what fuels my passion for cybersecurity.

> **"Caring is what fuels my passion for cybersecurity."**

You will never see sheepdogs worth their salt run from evil. In fact, they have been bred to confront evil head on. At the same time, you will never witness sheepdogs harming the sheep. In that sense, our information security sheepdogs are domesticated. They have had their aggression toward the sheep bred out of them. But when they see a wolf, it's game over.

How It Began

My entry into this world of sheepdogs, shepherds, and wolves happened almost by accident. After a three-year stint in an IT management role, I realized I had a knack for the bits and bytes of creating network infrastructure, so I started a consulting company to do just that. My first jobs, however, involved eradicating viruses and then applying protection to the machines so the infections wouldn't happen again. That is where my passion for security emerged.

One of the first companies I worked with was a previous client from my IT management days. We had a good relationship and the people trusted me. So when they had fifty machines behaving oddly, they called me.

I arrived armed with three McAfee programs that were new at the time: Scan, Clean, and V-Shield. I booted each machine by hand from a floppy disk with the Scan program installed. That, of course, ensured a clean environment, which led to the next step: determining which machines were infected. I then used Clean to eradicate the viruses. When I finished, I loaded V-Shield to keep each machine protected.

After that engagement, another organization approached me to do the same thing. Over time, more and more of my work focused on security and virus eradication. The need for such service was both obvious and overwhelming, so I decided to specialize in this area. I love serving people, so through that work I gained immense satisfaction from helping my clients improve their security stances from both physical *and* IT perspectives. I eliminated those threats with a sheepdog's mindset because wolves can quickly steal significant portions of a business. This has become even more imperative today as intellectual property is often an organization's greatest asset.

Over the years I've learned that a sheepdog's mindset is an encompassing worldview. It extends beyond a nine-to-five, Monday-through-Friday mindset into every facet of my life. It seems hard-wired into my DNA. Thus, no matter where I go, from a business environment to a restaurant with my family, I'm passionate about keeping the people I care about safe.

John's Leadership Perspective

Today I am a sheepdog. But I was once just one of the sheep, performing my role within the flock, unconcerned with larger dangers. When I transitioned to technology governance, risk management, and information security, I soon realized I needed to learn all four perspectives: that of the shepherd, the sheep, the sheepdog, and the wolf. I have served Fortune 50 companies in this capacity for more than twenty years. During that time, I began working with Jim, whose information security solutions and sheepdog mentality became a great help to me and the companies I served. His solution-oriented approach to collaborative selling and relationship building proved invaluable in helping me protect my flock from cyber threats. In many ways, Jim was the old sheepdog with a broad set of perspectives, tools, and experiences coming to help the younger sheepdog learn to better protect his flock.

As we begin this book, I want to start by helping you along the same path. When you work with sheepdogs like Jim, you can better understand their role and identify when they bring the right mindset to the table.

First, good sheepdogs will always put the flock above all else and will even sacrifice themselves for the benefit of the flock. But wolves consistently elevate their interests above everything and everyone else. The critical difference between the two is in their attitudes toward the sheep. There are five ways to measure and understand an effective sheepdog's security posture and mindset: *guide, guard, alert, respond, and rescue.*

> **"Good sheepdogs will always put the flock above all else and will even sacrifice themselves for the benefit of the flock."**

1. **Guide:** In cybersecurity, guiding is synonymous with education, training, and testing the sheep along the way.
2. **Guard:** The best sheepdogs guard their flocks by detecting threats and preventing security perimeter breaches. They do so by ensuring that the sheep

operate and remain in a safe environment with well-defined boundaries, both internal and external. Because the metaphor of sheep represents both the people and the assets of the organization, sheepdogs must adapt their guard strategy to fit the type of asset that needs protection.

3. **Alerts:** Sheepdogs always alert their shepherds when a threat is near. This means shepherds must listen carefully to the sheepdogs and heed their warnings. Effective organizational engagement and communication are essential for sheepdogs: if shepherds can't hear or understand their calls, their flocks will perish.

4. **Respond:** When a threat becomes imminent, the sheepdog must move from what Jim described as condition orange through condition red to condition black. This is an active engagement and mitigation of an active threat or intruder.

5. **Rescue:** Finally, quality sheepdogs rescue lost sheep. They find them and bring them back to the flock safely. This is the recovery after the incident: the process of returning the organization to condition yellow.

In addition to those five characteristics, it's also important to realize what a sheepdog's role is not. First, sheepdogs are not shepherds. Instead, they are an extension of the shepherd. This means that while sheepdogs play a substantive role in protecting their flocks, they are not ultimately responsible for their safety; rather, shepherds hold that ultimate accountability. This means shepherds must ensure that their sheepdogs have the security solutions, personnel, and organizational engagement they need to perform their roles effectively. Also paramount to understand is that as a business grows, so does its flock. So more than one sheepdog may be required to protect expanding assets. A symbiotic relationship exists between shepherd and sheepdog: the stronger that relationship is, the safer the sheep (assets, people, and intangibles such as the organization's reputation) will be.

Before we proceed, the most important thing to realize is that the sheep represent the whole of the organization. Sheep symbolize both the revenue-generating and the operational assets (human beings, information systems, intangibles) that can be compromised, lost, or stolen. When shepherds invest properly in security, they can tend to and guard the flock so that it has the space to grow and flourish. In sum, the sheep are the reason both shepherd and sheepdog exist. We will seek to foster this mindset through the rest of this book as we study effective sheepdogs and their strategies.

CHAPTER 2

HOW EFFECTIVE
SHEEPDOGS
THINK

I hope chapter one instilled just how important a sheepdog is to any organization with assets to protect. In this chapter, we'll take an even deeper look at how effective sheepdogs think. We will discover how interwoven logic and problem-solving approaches produce effective behavior. First, let's consider how the best sheepdogs think and behave so we can identify which ones will keep our sheep safe today and well into the future.

HOW GOOD SHEEPDOGS BEHAVE

The proper sheepdog mentality stems from an ability to see the big picture of an organization beyond day-to-day tasks. This means having a people- and relationships-first view of business. As a sheepdog, my approach is to build solid relationships with my clients as quickly as possible. To do my job well, I need to understand what keeps my clients up at night. What are their worries and fears? What are the problems they need to solve? How can I make sure I'm treating deeper issues rather than superficial symptoms?

From the beginning of my consultative sales career, I didn't charge for consultative services. I knew that as I understood my clients' problems, I would be able to bring the right solutions to the table. This is what sheepdogs continually need to do. It's not enough to throw a new solution at every new security threat that arises—that is a Band-Aid approach. Instead, we need to find both a cure *and* a means of prevention.

> **"To do my job well, I need to understand what keeps my clients up at night."**

When I founded my company, viruses were just starting to hit their stride. John McAfee had developed some of the most useful security solutions at the time, so I used them. And my clients followed suit, so much so that I attracted the attention of McAfee himself. In the spring of 1991, I answered the phone and was greeted by his gruff voice. My first thought was that I was in some serious trouble, that I must have done something *very* wrong. Instead of chewing me out, McAfee asked a litany of questions. He wanted to know more about what I was doing and how I was doing it.

I told him I was eradicating viruses using his security solutions and was experiencing great results. McAfee already knew that because everywhere I went, people were ordering his software after the free thirty-day shareware trial expired. Because I was a consultant for those clients, John knew that my income would always be limited by the hours I could bill, so he offered me the first partner deal McAfee had ever made; it was called the Authorized Agents Program. All I had to do was give McAfee a call and let him know where I had installed his software. Then, if my customer placed a software order, McAfee would cut me a check. It only took two months for me to see financial remuneration from that new model, and I quickly realized I could make *a lot* of money selling, rather than trading my time for money.

But the sheepdog in me didn't want to lose my consultative approach. I didn't want to come in with my antivirus guns blazin' and try to sell products before I really understood my clients' issues. I still wanted to see their problems solved and prevented, so my approach evolved into the consultative sales approach I still use today. I view myself as a partner first, one who seeks to understand an organization's security postures. My goal is to help identify the chinks in the security environment's armor. Only after I've discovered the gaps do I address them with the right solutions. In all, this produces consistent win-wins for my clients and my company.

HEALTH CHECKS, MINDSETS, AND OLD SHEEPDOGS

Implementing solutions like these is one of my favorite activities. But, as a sheepdog, I know that my work will never be done, and neither will my client's. As we'll discuss in the next chapter, today's cybersecurity landscape is shifting at such an incredible rate that it's not enough to deploy a few security solutions and then move on. I view every security solution I sell, install, and support as an *ongoing* commitment to my customer. That is why I conduct consistent information security health checks with all my clients. An information security strategy needs constant review and visitation, so we do that together—and to great effect.

Through my relationships with my vendors, I have been able to exponentially increase my ability to protect clients. The solutions I leave behind extend my guarding reach. I've also increased my business by partnering with likeminded people rather than pushing an ever-greater catalog of products. This sheepdog mentality of providing ongoing solutions through a consultative sales approach is ingrained in every member of my team.

I am bringing these points up not to sell to you but to educate you about how to go through a discovery process of your own. This will help you uncover your true needs rather than running through box after box of Band-Aids and extinguishing constant fires. When you approach problems with a consultative, sheepdog mindset, you can solve them today and prevent them tomorrow. But most importantly, *when* a breach eventually occurs, you will be prepared to execute the proper response. This approach has helped me consistently present solutions that work, scale well, and keep my clients safe.

This drive started early in life with my favorite book, *The Way Things Work.* I've always had a hunger to understand everything from what makes clocks tick to what makes processors spin, and I've found that this curious and investigative nature makes great sheepdogs.

"This will help you uncover your true needs rather than running through box after box of Band-Aids and extinguishing constant fires."

This attitude manifests itself in many ways, most often in lines of inquiry.

For instance, when I am called about ransomware I don't start trying to sell our next-generation antimalware solution. Rather, I ask, "Why is this ransomware so bad for your organization?" The answer may appear obvious, but it invites a deeper understanding of the organization as a whole. For instance, it may be a HIPAA/HITECH compliance issue. From there, we can identify not only the assets that have been taken hostage, but other facets of the organization that also may be vulnerable.

Untrained sheepdogs don't ask questions like those. That's why bringing in an older sheepdog to guide one who is new to the position can make all the difference in the world. If you can, always invest in a battle-hardened sheepdog to train a younger one. That way, the new sheepdog can learn and implement the right mentality and behaviors from day one.

John's Leadership Perspective

Jim is a wise old sheepdog who has dealt with many threats. I think of him as a trainer who keeps both shepherd and sheepdog effective by helping them work together more effectively. As a sheepdog myself, I've taken a cue from him and always start with the question rather than the solution.

With that mentality, I've been able to align security strategies with business strategies rather than merely implementing technologies to fill the gaps. The best sheepdogs don't simply plug holes: we partner, collaborate, and maintain a consultative nature that allows us to understand our organization's functional maturity in cybersecurity. Then we can take out our solution sets and customize unique and tailored security solutions to address the threats we face.

During my tenure, I tended to build exclusive relationships with a few vendors. I looked for the rare breed of sheepdog, and I found one in Jim. He never jumped straight to the sales pitch or line card, he never attempted to over-engineer a solution, and he never underengineered in hopes of a quick sale. Rather, he brought a collaborative spirit that was much like Goldilocks: *not too hot, not too cold, but just right*, never stopping at the sale or implementation of the solution. Like the vigilant sheepdog, Jim was always available and provided a critical interface between me and the product suppliers on whom I relied to protect my flock.

That approach distinguished Jim from the many predatory sales people, often disguised as sheepdogs, who only wanted to make a quick sale and move on. When you do what Jim and I have done, you build a genuine personal relationship beyond the business relationship and discover what I call the "lagging indicator" of a genuine sheepdog. When you've implemented a successful solution, you will return time and again to the sheepdog that helped you craft it. These are the sheepdogs worth partnering with and emulating because they are the ones who ultimately keep your sheep secure and your flock safe.

CHAPTER 3

THE EVOLVING LANDSCAPE OF CYBERSECURITY

E ffective sheepdogs will continue to grow in importance to their organization as their technology environment changes. Although cybersecurity has changed dramatically, there are still success factors to strive for and warning signs to be wary of. In this chapter, John and I will outline some notable success indicators as well as red flags, and then John will provide an overview of the role of today's CISOs and how they can be most effective within their organizations. First, let's explore the critical success factors of operational IT security.

CRITICAL SUCCESS FACTORS
OF OPERATIONAL IT SECURITY

A familiar metaphor in cybersecurity is the "three-legged stool" that represents people, process, and controls. One of the success factors of operational IT security is that those three legs are aligned and working together. Every organization has people, but those people must be working with defined processes and, as verification that said processes are being followed, they must be implementing the right controls. This allows an organization to deter-

> **"If a coordinated strategy is not in place, there will be unanticipated vulnerabilities."**

mine two things: (1) whether its people are following their processes, and (2) if they are not complying with those processes, ensuring that bad things won't happen. Our role is to help determine where organizations are in this process. But an overarching strategy must drive each of these components. This is a prime function for any sheepdog because if a coordinated strategy is not in place, there will be unanticipated vulnerabilities. To develop a strategic vision for an organization's security, a sheepdog must first determine where those vulnerabilities are and determine the risk each vulnerability poses to the flock. As the saying goes, we need to walk before we can run. And where security is concerned, that means arriving at a genuine awareness of the flock's current state.

A sheepdog assesses that by answering questions such as, "What is our capacity for accepting risk with the absence of mitigation?" In essence, what potential vulnerabilities has the organization's shepherd determined acceptable without a dedicated solution in place? Another simple but critical question is this: "What budget do we have?" Is the cybersecurity budget simply a facet of the organization's IT budget as a whole, or are resources allocated specifically for it? After all, if the security budget is underfunded, then every stakeholder needs to be aware of the risk factors inherent in such a budget. As you can see, this question correlates directly with the first question because an underfunded security budget means that the organization is accepting risks, acknowledged or not, which also has a direct impact on operations.

Operations

From our perspective, an organization must incorporate any solution we offer into its operations. Otherwise, we're selling "shelfware," which isn't much help to anyone. When sheepdogs fail to incorporate our solutions into their companies' ongoing operations, they actually realize a negative value. Long term, this means that our relationship won't be nearly as strong and that our customer isn't benefiting from its investment. The organization must operationalize these expenditures to get anything out of them: after all, the intent is to stop sensitive assets from heading out the door. Therefore, when an organization doesn't adopt solutions as a part of its overall strategy, the value of its assets decreases significantly.

Speed

Just as critical to operationalizing our solutions is rapid deployment. When an organization spends money on a product, the quicker it puts the product to use, the quicker it realizes positive value. This is why one of our key principles is lightning-fast "time-to-value." In other words, we want every sheepdog to see results and benefit as quickly as possible from the investment. The longer a solution takes to implement, the longer an organization takes to benefit. Most of our solutions demonstrate this quick time-to-value during the evaluation or proof of concept phase. Solutions also must enable the responder to engage the threat rapidly and effectively before a loss occurs. If solutions are too complicated, the sheepdog will never be able to keep up with the wolf.

Data Analytics

One of the prime factors in rapid time-to-value is understanding which data to focus on in any given situation. As you well know, today's tools spit out streams of information and analytics. By and large, this is great. The more information the better, right? While this is true, if data is unfiltered, sheepdogs will end up with a deluge of information. In reality, this can result in a tool that produces more white noise than insight. Our approach then is to recommend a solution that correlates the results of the output of all active security products that the organization has operationalized. This provides valuable insight into relevant data, which is pivotal because effective sheepdogs focus on the right events in real time.

John's Leadership Perspective

OUTSOURCING SECURITY: THE BENEFITS

Security organizations struggle to maintain the balance between deploying all the tools necessary to protect the environment and having enough human capital to operate them. The final success factor in analyzing your security posture is considering how to best augment your existing human capability through strategic outsourcing of key components of your program to managed service providers. When considering any outsourcing initiative, one needs to assess the benefits and drawbacks of doing so. One of the biggest benefits to working with a managed security services provider (MSSP) is that you do not have to increase headcount to increase security. This means that you can employ super sheepdogs whose specialty lies in analyzing security incidents. Also, an MSSP allows for an operational budget expense rather than technology and human capital investments. Overall, this can make quality 24/7 monitoring a reality for some companies while minimizing headcount and compensation increases.

Outsourcing Security: The Caution Flag

Outsourcing's drawbacks can counterbalance its benefits. First among these is the classic principle of "garbage in, garbage out". If you are feeding your MSSP unfiltered data, it will only be able to generate more noise. That wastes money on multiple levels and may lead to serious security threats going unnoticed because they are buried in millions of events happening at any given time. To counteract that possibility, events need to be filtered down to the ten or twenty that are critical. That filtering is hard work, but it must be done for the investment to pay off. In addition, those events should be revisited every two to four weeks. In those meetings, you will be able to further refine and filter what's most important. As a leader, you can't just throw your garbage over the wall and expect it not to smell. Before outsourcing, you must spend the time to understand the data and create rules that establish what data is truly relevant and under what conditions. Then you must plan to invest significant time in your MSSP to bring relevance and perspective to the employees who service your account.

An MSSP will never know your business as well as you do. So if you do not invest sufficient time in the MSSP relationship, it will ultimately fail. The goal should be to make the MSSP indistinguishable from an employee in your organization. This relationship should be viewed as a partnership rather than as a vendor agreement.

"This relationship should be viewed as a partnership rather than as a vendor agreement."

Your IT security team needs to be right 100,000 times out of 100,000 because the one time when it isn't will be the one time you get breached. I tell my companies and clients that the secret to operational security isn't understanding the tool; rather, it's understanding the data beneath the tool and learning how to identify minute changes in flock behavior that signal an impending attack. If you are willing to invest in data analytics and apply that to your service providers, you will find an MSSP to be a valuable tool.

THE ROLE OF THE CISO:
THE INTERNAL SHEEPDOG

Now that we have cataloged some of the critical success factors in IT security today, let's take a look at how the role of the CISO has evolved. The old model of security was: *build a firewall because everything outside our organization's environment is bad and untrustworthy, and everything inside it is good and safe.* The mindset was that the only real threats came from external actors— the wolves—making inroads *into* the organization. That mindset meant that everyone inside the organization— the flock—could be trusted. Worse yet, the leaders and shepherds had grown complacent. In fact, many leaders didn't even have sheepdogs; they merely had fences, walls, and a belief that their environment would tend to itself. But the outside-versus-inside mentality has become irrelevant because everything on both sides of the firewall has become interconnected. The network perimeter has vanished.

Historically, shepherds have trusted their sheep to self-regulate—but remember, sheep aren't simply the employees. Our metaphorical sheep are also an organization's assets including intellectual properties and all else that makes a business uniquely valuable. Today, those well-defined fences of separation are gone. But leaders often have struggled to understand that information cannot be trusted to stay secure; thus, the "zero-trust model" was born.

This model did not develop from a fundamental lack of trust between an organization's leadership and its employees. Rather, in today's digital landscape, sheepdogs cannot be certain that the person logging into a workstation is genuinely the same person whose credentials are being input to gain access. In simple terms, bad actors steal usernames and passwords, so a user's authenticity cannot always be verified. This means that the wolves prowl inside the fence too.

Today, employees work on smartphones and personal devices of all kinds. Where are those devices often located? They are well beyond the protective bounds of the organization's fence. In effect, the smartphone has destroyed the perimeter. With wolves all around, assets are in greater danger now than ever. But an organization's leaders are still responsible for the security of those assets. A breach is extremely costly at all levels and, as we have shown, the risks keep escalating. For the shepherds, though, the result is a landscape in which a good sheepdog has preeminent value. For shepherds who are responsible for all of their companies' assets, a CISO who understands both security *and* business needs is the new model for leadership in cybersecurity.

The Old Model

It is safe to say that the CISO's traditional role is outmoded. In the recent past, the average CISO came from an infrastructure or information technology background and, with a promotion or title change, suddenly gained responsibility for an organization's security. This new sheepdog understood tech but was untrained. Even worse, this fresh-off-the-bus CISO brought along an IT mindset but not a business one. And that is an issue because the CISO is responsible for the business as a whole, not just for its IT. This is a fundamental shift in how technology and security leaders see their roles.

That's why today's sheepdogs need a business savvy they may not have needed until now. This business acumen enables the CISOs to walk alongside their organizations' leadership as both an advisor *and* watchdog. In turn, this means that shepherds—from CEOs to boards of directors—need to care about *and* listen to their sheepdogs if they want to be well advised and enabled to lead. The business side of an organization is no longer separate from its internal, technical side. An organization's technology infrastructure doesn't simply enable its employees to do the work that adds value; it is now part of the value itself.

Today's CISOs understand this but, to be effective, they must have influence beyond a simple section of the sheep. Previously, the thinking was, "Well, they are IT people, so they're limited to IT concerns and stay within the CIO's boundaries. Their only concern is for that section of the sheep over there." Instead, the sheep-dog exists for all of the sheep and must be understood as the shepherd's right hand in protecting the organization's assets. One way a CISO can do this is by forming a steering committee with other key business leaders that will help guide cybersecurity and reporting. From there, the CISO also can take an active role as a permanent member of the organization's risk committee. The sheepdog can then advise the organization's leaders on cybersecurity risk and contribute from a business perspective as well. One of the prime ways to do this is by understanding the threat landscape beyond the sheepdog's own organization.

The Networked CISO

To achieve this broader perspective, I am a firm believer in the value of a networked CISO. Sheepdogs that form a strategic peer network will prove invaluable because they can collect intelligence from the group. Therefore, if the sheepdog of the flock in the next field barks and says, "There are wolves about, and here is how they are trying to get in," the other sheepdogs can be on alert for that specific threat. In essence, well-networked sheepdogs can apply the security acumen of an entire community to their organization's information security.

If your sheepdog focuses only on your own flock, your organization may be unprepared for the threat in the next field. But when CISOs share collaborative experience, the entire industry improves faster and everyone benefits. I've seen this many times when working with Jim because he works with so many other sheepdogs: as threats surface, his intelligence network sharpens his insight.

Relationships and Presence

The best sheepdogs, then, will have well-rounded relational abilities. From internal relationships and committees to the peer networks we have just discussed, CISOs need to be excellent communicators and leaders. Thus, a business leader should look for a CISO who has a technology background but who is not a technologist: in other words, a CISO with an executive presence. This is key because the CISO must approach cybersecurity as a facet of the business as a revenue-protecting and revenue-generating organization. That also means the CISO will have the ability to engage the organization at the appropriate level. It's difficult for the average network engineer to brief and relate to a C-level person when it comes to the business implications of cybersecurity.

A sales approach characterized by questions such as "What is keeping you up at night?", "What are the problems you're trying to solve right now?", "What risks are you concerned about?", and "Can I help you understand them better?" works well when interacting with these sheepdogs. This approach is radically different from one in which resellers promote themselves or a product. This consultative sales approach will allow the CISO to achieve both business goals and security goals at the same time. I call this persuasive pragmatism because it stems from a mindset that prioritizes risk and risk tolerance rather than merely implementing security solutions.

HOW TO EMPOWER THE CISO

Nonetheless, the best sheepdogs are only effective to the degree that they are empowered by an organization's leadership. There are many ways to provide that empowerment, but the two we will consider here are unfiltered organizational access and a separate budget. These will enable your sheepdog to be successful, which means your organization will have a greater chance of success as a whole.

First, then, it is important to give the CISO unfiltered organizational access. What I mean is that the CISO cannot be bound by the normal chain of command. CISOs must have access to the right people or their effectiveness will be limited. I have spoken with the head of the Securities and Exchange Commission (SEC) and the operational head of the FBI and they each identified the same red-flag indicator: when they go into an organization and the board, CEO, or president has never talked directly to the CISO or head of security. When this is the case, a change is in order if you want to keep your sheep as secure as possible.

Second, sheepdogs should have distinct budgets to avoid diluting their priorities. The CIO should not be deciding what the CISO can spend. Instead, the board should determine that figure and allocate a separate budget. The reason for doing so is as much for the shepherd's benefit as it is for the sheepdog's. Shepherds bear the ultimate responsibility for compliance and security in their organizations.

When the sheepdogs can propose their own budgets, the risk committees—of which the CISOs should also be members—will validate it by performing a risk analysis. This will provide concrete reasons for proposed spending in the coming budget cycle. The dollars won't simply be for the newest product but for solutions proposed within the risk tolerance that the shepherds have deemed acceptable to their organizations. Every dollar is then tied to mitigating the risk upon which everyone has agreed, and this risk is ever present when wolves are around. Today, this risk is there all the time and in every place, so that is the topic of our next chapter.

PART TWO

STRENGTHEN

CHAPTER 4

THE WOLVES

F rom the Target hack of 2013 that resulted in the theft of millions of credit cards to the JP Morgan Chase breach that was the largest-ever theft of customer data from an American financial institution,[1] high-profile hacks and data breaches are on the rise. But the little-understood truth is that the risk is not limited to governments and billion-dollar corporations. Today, anyone with a personal or business relationship or data with even a shred of value is under threat. If you recall our analogy of the pasture, there were four primary

---

[1]"JP Morgan's Accused Hackers Had Vast $100 Million Operation," *CNN Money*, November 10, 2015. http://money.cnn.com/2015/11/10/technology/jpmorgan-hack-charges/index.html.

characters: the shepherd, the sheepdog, the sheep, and the wolves. Wolves come in many colors, and each has a different motivation. In this chapter, we will identify what today's wolves are after and then we will expose a specific hidden threat that often goes unnoticed until it's too late.

THE RED WOLF

Let's begin with the red wolf. This wolf symbolizes unfriendly governments and their military-like exploits. Whether the nation-state in question is China, North Korea, Russia, or any other, they all have a similar agenda: they attack companies and governments alike to gather intelligence and extort money from those entities. And red wolves employ a new method of warfare with nationalistic motivations that range from election disruption to espionage.

> **"They attack companies and governments alike to gather intelligence and extort money from those entities."**

Red wolves are excellent at what they do; they are well trained and work with almost unlimited resources. As a result, they can attack from sophisticated equipment backed by substantial budgets, and each will use a different method to attack your infrastructure. Some are direct, brute-force hacks of firewalls while others are much more elaborate and use social engineering. In the latter case, the red wolves craft subtle ways to hack organizations. For example, they may do extensive research into an organization and find its key players. From there, the red wolves make an email look as if it is coming internally from a specific person. For instance, a CEO may be sending an email to the CFO requesting that funds be transferred to a specific bank account; however, the CEO isn't really the one doing the asking.

While this type of attack isn't unique to red wolves, it is a great example of their intimate knowledge of their targets. But thankfully, the red wolves also have weaknesses. First among them is that when an attack occurs, you can usually identify where it originated from geographically. This means that you can quickly determine which country or government you are dealing with. The key takeaway is that red wolves are well equipped, well trained, well paid, and motivated by nationalistic goals. These factors combine to make the red wolf a potent enemy, but not an impossible one.

THE GRAY WOLF

Next is the gray wolf, otherwise known as a "hacktivist." These are black-hat hackers whose motivation is to upset the proverbial applecart—in other words, they are anarchists. While their goal may seem similar to that of the red wolves, gray wolves aren't loyal to a specific nation. In fact, their associations are generally quite loose. Groups like Anonymous are gray wolves. They pursue their own mission for their own reasons—sometimes for little more than proving they can breach a powerful organization. Take, for instance, the incident in early 2012 when the CIA's public-facing homepage was replaced by political hactivists.

Gray wolves are technically astute and intelligent, but they are often unfunded. However, that is what is peculiar about them; they generally work for a political or social goal rather than a monetary one. For example, WikiLeaks has a stated goal of gathering information for the greater good. Even though gray wolves are not engaged in national acts of war, they still pose serious threats to both government and private sector organizations.

THE WHITE WOLF

Next is the white wolf, a threat that few discuss. This wolf is a friendly government gathering intelligence on its own people through surveillance. For instance, there have been a number of investigations into the NSA's data collection activities and capabilities. While we may be sympathetic to our own government, we also must be cautious to protect against its potential exploitation of power in a manner similar to that of a rogue government. US government surveillance methods include monitoring and recording phone calls, text messages, emails, and more. In coming years, it will be increasingly important for companies to be aware of these white wolves.

And the mantle of the white wolf extends beyond US borders. White wolves can be any of our allies or other friendly governments, but that does not mean they aren't dangerous. For whatever reason, they are collecting intelligence on the private sector without permission. And governments don't always stay friendly forever: a nation who is our ally today may be interested in future-proofing itself by mining data from a friendly country's marketplace.

The assets white wolves are after could be anything from employee records to intellectual property, but even though they are wearing white hats, they are not always on our side. Every country's first motivation will be its own protection and gain. Thus, like red wolves, white wolves have nearly unlimited access to funds and resources to perform their tasks in addition to legal and governmental powers to gain additional access they would not otherwise have.

Even so, white wolves with all their resources have a major weakness: they rely on secrecy to conduct their operations and are vulnerable to whistleblowers and watchdogs. Edward Snowden ended up being a threat by exposing the white wolf when he publicized government operations, effecting political change by flipping the popular sentiment that the government is doing nothing but good on its head. Suddenly, the public realized that it had become the victim of its own government's snooping. This weakness goes even deeper when the intelligence leaked is sensitive to national security—protecting troops on the battlefield, for example. I'm not suggesting that sheepdogs wear tinfoil hats, but they must be aware that white wolves pose a threat. So sheepdogs must consider steps to prevent intrusive data mining and collection.

THE BLACK WOLF

If the white wolf is the least discussed, the black wolf has the highest profile. The motive of black wolves is simple and unsurprising: they are in it for the money. They are looking for power and leverage to extort money from individuals and organizations. They will sell access and information on the dark web or any other criminal network after they have gained access to that information. The operative word is "sell." Black wolves are looking to hold information hostage for profit.

But the weakness of black wolves lies primarily in their levels of sophistication and predictability. They are always after the low-hanging fruit because they are the least technically savvy of the entire pack. Black wolves will use off-the-shelf malware that has been repackaged repeatedly. Their level of technical expertise is low because their primary methods simply don't need deep sophistication. These are the smash-and-grab criminals who run up to the jewelry store, bust the front window display, and then make off with the loot as fast as they can.

> **"Black wolves are looking to hold information hostage for profit."**

The JP Morgan "pump-and-dump" breach that we referenced at the beginning of the chapter is an excellent example of a black wolf attack. In this case, three men breached the financial giant's defenses and stole the personal data of over 80 million customers. The attack was a coordinated effort that sent misleading emails to encourage people to buy stocks the criminals had purchased for pennies and would then sell at an inflated price before the stock price tumbled back to the bottom. While black wolves may employ more simplistic tactics, they are no less dangerous or destructive than the other wolves.

Now that we have discussed the four primary colors of wolves, John is going to unveil the hidden threat that lurks inside the fence. This secret wolf could be of any color, but it will hide in plain sight. I'm talking about the wolf in sheep's clothing. This wolf walks, talks, and acts like the other sheep, and that is why it is so dangerous.

John's Leadership Perspective

THE WOLF IN SHEEP'S CLOTHING

In some ways, I think of this as the ghost wolf. And it is arguably the most dangerous because this wolf sits inside your fences without your even knowing it's there. Its motivations could be those of any of the other wolves because it can be any of them. Whether it is engaging in espionage, prowling for financial gain, or motivated by activism or even altruism, it is there to steal right in front of your eyes.

Most often, these wolves started as sheep but became corrupted. Some outside force influenced them enough to change their thinking and behavior. Those influences may be the desire for money or any other manner of personal gain. But no matter what, these wolves are after your data. They often will strike within about two weeks of giving their notice to leave the organization. This could mean that they are taking customer lists or physical devices with poor asset management or even making copies of trade secrets. I think these are the most dangerous wolves because they capitalize on the "trust everybody on the inside" mentality. Leaders who still see their companies from that perspective often struggle with the practice of employee surveillance. But this trust is precisely what makes this wolf so effective and dangerous.

> **"They are taking customer lists or physical devices with poor asset management or even making copies of trade secrets."**

Unfortunately, shepherds trust these wolves and often give them more access to sensitive data than they need to do their jobs. Only after it is too late can the organization identify their activities. In fact, I remember talking to an HR person who performed an exit interview of an employee only to discover that the person had taken a copy of an entire customer database so he could use it while working for a competitor. What a lucky break! But what about all of the rest who don't have a compulsion to confess? CISOs need a trust-but-verify mindset to prevail; and just like the sheepdog, they need to sniff out the wolves trying to attack their sheep.

Sheepdogs always need to be on the hunt for behavioral abnormalities. The triggers can be subtle or obvious: logging in at an odd time of night, downloading a large volume of documents, or suddenly browsing job sites. A good sheepdog is aware of the reality that not only do wolves infiltrate the flock, but sometimes the sheep decide to take on the role of wolves—and you will never know when this will happen. You cannot distinguish between the outside of the fence and the inside or between the bad and the good. With everything intermingled, the zero-trust mentality is critical. Zero trust is the most misunderstood term among the shepherds, the management of the organization. It sounds bad; it sounds wrong. But zero trust doesn't mean that we inherently mistrust people. Rather, it implies that we inherently don't know if the identity of the person acting as a sheep is true. Again, we have to sniff it out and make sure it has been a sheep and still is a sheep.

Additionally, sheepdogs must understand that no organization is too small to be under threat. I have sat with many leaders who have said, "The Chinese would never care about us. We don't have anything of value to them." But what leaders with this mentality miss is that *any* intelligence is valuable to an adversary. This intelligence is not simply limited to what you have; it also consists of your connections to other organizations. Wolves will attack one sheep as a diversion and then go after the real target. To which companies or government organizations could you serve as a gateway? Can they exploit you to gain access to the real target? For instance, how many board members have close relationships with other organization's boards or CEOs?

THE GATEWAY TO THE BREACH

One of the best examples of this is the 2013 Target breach that Jim referenced at the beginning of the chapter. From Thanksgiving to Christmas 2013, hackers gained access to millions of credit cards and other personal information. Target was breached; not directly, but through its relationship with an HVAC company.

Target's HVAC network and IT network were connected, which resulted in a total breach of operational controls. The networks were supposed to be separate with each inaccessible from the other. But someone gained access to a user ID and password of an HVAC account in the Target domain and, from there, the hacker accessed operational point-of-sale devices in each store and seeded them with malware.

Target's vulnerability resulted from a vendor inadvertently serving as a gateway into their fold. How many air conditioning companies think they have any data assets of value? Probably not many. But the truth is that relationships are just as valuable, if not more so. Access has always been and always will be the keys to the kingdom for the bad actors. That means you can never assume you are not at risk because when you embrace that mindset, you become more vulnerable than ever. That is why sheepdogs must be ever vigilant if they are going to keep the wolves out.

CHAPTER 5

KEEPING
THE WOLVES OUT

N ow that you know the story and the actors, let's venture into your organization's security strategy. When I work with companies, I help employ a multilayered approach that takes into account all of the variables we have uncovered so far. In our analogy of the pasture, the old wooden fence represents the old-world security strategy. That thinking was based on keeping the bad stuff outside at bay and the good stuff inside protected. But as we have demonstrated, that strategy won't cut it anymore.

CONCENTRIC FENCES

In the old world, we based security on an outside-in perspective. But in the new world, we need an inside-out strategy to be effective against today's wolves. I call this the "concentric fences" approach. Imagine a series of concentric circles in which a large outer circle encompasses incrementally smaller circles. Each circle represents a layer of defense against the wolves. But as they grow smaller, they become progressively stronger—or taller—as you move toward the center where the sheep are. Therefore, the outer layer is the lowest or weakest fence, and the center layer is the highest or most fortified. The old model simply employed the large outer circle—the firewall. Thus, the concentric-fences approach represents a departure from the old world, a multilayered defense engineered precisely for today's cybersecurity environment. In this model, we need to build five fences. Listing them from the outside in, they are *physical, network, devices, users,* and *assets.*

> **"A multilayered defense engineered precisely for today's cybersecurity environment."**

1. **Physical:** The first layer is a facility's physical security. Examples of the physical security layer include security cameras, parking lot gates, physical fences, man traps, locks, access control badges, security guards, and any other physical component of security.

2. **Network:** The second layer is your network—the way that your devices exchange data both inside and outside your network. This is where firewalls form the fence of demarcation, the point where your internal network ends and the greater Internet begins. This fence controls the flow of data in and out of your organization. Here you also will find intrusion detection and prevention systems, data loss prevention (DLP), and network layers. As an example, your DLP solution could detect information associated with a credit card number trying to leave your network and stop it in its tracks. It could also detect and stop that type of data from entering your network and help you educate your customers that they are sending this data to your organization insecurely across the Internet. Essentially, this layer

guards against any threats or suspicious activity at the organizational network level.

3. **Devices:** The third layer protects any device attached to your network including desktops, laptops, smart phones, file servers, tablets, and even printers.

4. **Users:** The fourth layer is also the largest variable: your people. I call this the "un-patchable" component because the sheepdog can never rely on people to do the right thing by default. That is why we train people; they are the greatest risk and weakest link of all—not because of any lack of intelligence but because they are simply trying to do their jobs. That makes them prime attack targets.

5. **Assets:** Finally, the fifth layer protects the assets themselves. These are the data, information, or intellectual property that the wolves are ultimately after. This is the strongest and tallest layer of our concentric fences and lies at the heart of everything. Think of this as the impenetrable castle wall, the encryption or data firewall that is the last line of defense. In essence, we are equipping sheep with Kevlar vests because the zeroes-and-ones are where the value is.

THE LAYERS IN PRACTICE

Now, let's put our fences to the test with a real-world example. Imagine that a data packet is coming from outside our organization to the inside. It first must pass through the firewall, the lowest fence. The next fence will be stronger and may be something like DLP. But because the data flows both ways, the DLP perimeter is built around the path of the data itself that controls its flow and use. The nuance of this approach is that the fences aren't simply built around an organization but around the assets. Our layering has to go where the data goes. But as we've already discussed, the data doesn't stay within the fences any longer. It is on phones, laptops, and other devices being used in coffee shops, homes, and other businesses.

Ultimately, what we are trying to do is protect the soft underbelly of the organization because that is what the wolves are after. To further protect our data, we should focus on the people component of the three-legged stool. We need to educate and train people to be wiser and more security-conscious. We need our sheep to follow best practices and our sheepdogs to be more effective, alert, and well networked. In all, we need to trust but verify that our employees are following the processes and procedures laid out to keep our assets secure. When we couple that training with the right security solutions, we can prevent many bad things from happening yet still have a plan for when they do.

The crux of this concentric circles paradigm is to guard from the inside out, starting with the lowest common denominator: user workstations or devices. This is where users read and respond to email, log in and out of internal systems, and where the majority of business activity happens. So this is where the wolves are most likely to attack and where the risk is the greatest. That is why we have high fences in the center, the endpoint. Wolves are not breaking through firewalls anymore because they don't need to. They only need to reach the user who has a key to every door the wolves want to sneak through.

John's Leadership Perspective

The US's National Cyber Security Alliance found that 60 percent of small companies go out of business within six months after a cyberattack. Additionally, the Ponemon Institute identified the average price for middle-market companies to recover from a breach to be in excess of one million dollars. Thus, to take an outmoded approach to protecting against breaches is a dereliction of duty to our organizations. We need to be pragmatic and thoughtful in our cybersecurity strategy. From shepherd to sheepdog, we owe our investors, our shareholders, and our employees our best effort in protecting the organization's assets. To do that well, every CISO needs a risk matrix written from a business perspective.

THE RISK MATRIX

Every conversation a CISO has when talking about cybersecurity should be in the context of risk. The purpose of the risk matrix is to list the threats facing an organization, the likelihood that they will happen, and the overall impact if they do occur (financially, gravitationally, organizationally, etc.) The risk matrix quantifies an organization's risk. When done well, this matrix will encompass a 360-degree perspective, meaning that all business decisions can be based upon and informed by it. Once it is in place, it will drive investments in the controls that we will discuss further in the next chapter.

The reason formalizing risk acceptance is so important is that so many organizations only do this informally. When acceptable risk is undocumented, organizations are surprised when disaster strikes because they never comprehended the risk they had tacitly accepted. Yet again, this is why the shepherds must be the ones who determine what level of risk to take on. Passive acceptance is not enough to ensure that assets are safe. In fact, an organization's security strategy must incorporate even accepted risks. Simply deeming a risk acceptable does not mean not accounting for it. The best practice is to review the risk matrix periodically and revisit which risks are still acceptable and which are not. For every unacceptable risk, you must have an action plan to address the risk in a timely manner. Action plans must be aligned to the risk matrix and implemented timely based on risk tolerance. They must have the ultimate goal to implement controls and measures that sufficiently mitigate the impact to the organization in the event an identified risk becomes actualized.

THE EASIEST RISK TO OVERLOOK

The easiest risk to overlook is the users because they are the least configurable of all the layers. It is difficult to automatically correct your employees' behaviors and decision making. After all, 95 percent of data breaches are from either an intentional or unintentional user action that compromises security.[2] For instance, your people handle data every day and it is too easy for them to forget to send it securely. It also makes it easier for the wolves in sheep's clothing to steal assets.

It bears reiterating that training, educating, and watching users across the board is vital to any security strategy. To neglect that is unacceptable risk. In my experience, this is the most under-invested segment of cybersecurity. As the CISO, begin with users to ensure you have the right people, processes, and model before you invest in security solutions. You should make an equal or even greater investment in training the technologists who will be responsible for operationalizing the security solutions you purchase. The total cost of a security solution must include both the purchase price and the training for internal teams to

> **"To neglect that is unacceptable risk. In my experience, this is the most under-invested segment of cybersecurity."**

---

[2] "2014 Cyber Security Intelligence Index" IBM, Date 12/5/2016, https://media.scmagazine.com/documents/82/ibm_cyber_security_intelligenc_20450.pdf

use it. If you do not have people who understand the data that the solution creates, you will never realize value. This is why the best CISOs run cybersecurity like a business. If they cannot demonstrate value through metrics, both the security and the strategy will be irrelevant.

In summary, the risk matrix is an essential tool for sheepdogs that enables them to incorporate, engage, and educate the shepherd and the flock while maintaining relevance and ensuring that security solutions align with the organization's overall strategy and risk tolerance. A control without an understanding of the risk is useless because you do not know what you are solving. When you don't know the objective, you have no ability to measure its efficacy. But a well-formed action plan is the manifestation of risk-management and drives the controls that you establish, which the next chapter will further explore.

PART THREE

PREPARE
AND RESPOND

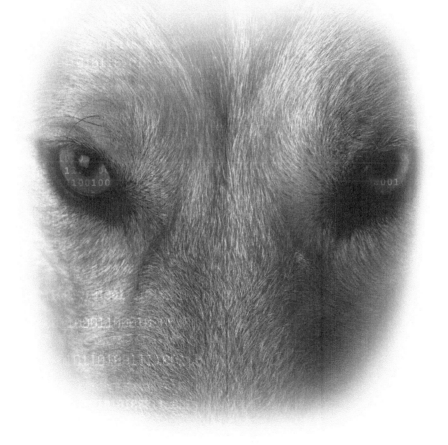

CHAPTER 6

CONTROLLING WOLVES AND SHEEP

W hen you do not control your sheep's behavior, the wolves sneak in. To ensure security, you must establish the right controls. But because no single control can be 100 percent effective, you must assume a defense-in-depth mentality. The line we will walk in this chapter is to understand the essential controls without over-engineering a solution. To accomplish that, we will seek to "allow the good rather than look for the bad". In other words, we focus on what actions we need to take for employees to perform their jobs well rather than to account for every possible attack scenario.

A control is a process or technology that establishes the boundaries of good behavior versus bad and defines the limits on a given stream of action. For any risk that an organization chooses not to accept, these boundaries are put in place to mitigate it. A control, then, enforces a policy statement or risk posture an organization has adopted. For example, the policy may be that users must change their password every ninety days. The control is what forces this to happen. It can either be human or technology-based. In all, a control is the manifestation of an organization's risk appetite that sets the limits on acceptable behavior.

CONTROLS AND FRAMEWORKS

When you have a defined set of controls, you also have limits. In turn, you can control the consistency of a policy's application. To set the right controls and frameworks, here is the progression:

1. **Risk Appetite:** Define your organization's risk appetite.

2. **Policies and Procedures:** Create your policies and procedures based upon acceptable and unacceptable risk.

3. **Controls:** Implement controls that will enforce the consistent application of the policies and procedures above.

4. **Frameworks:** Select a framework that will assess the effectiveness of said controls.

A framework is a set of controls used to gauge your program's maturity and effectiveness. A number of good frameworks are available, including the National Institute of Standards and Technology (NIST), International Organization for Standardization (ISO), or the Payment Card Industry Data Security Standard (PCI DSS). But more important than the specific framework you use is the fact that you have one. If your organization were a football team, your framework would be the game plan.

> **"A framework is a set of controls used to gauge your program's maturity and effectiveness."**

YOUR CRITICAL CATEGORIES

When defining controls, you must consider five key areas of risk mitigation: *tailored education of users, privileged access management (PAM), classification and identification of data, segregation of critical assets and users,* and *incident response and recovery.* We will discuss the importance of each and then we will offer some final advice on implementing them. Let's start with your users.

One: Training Users

Every organization should have an end-user training program that also incorporates ongoing testing. It's important for training to go beyond the bounds of a single session or security workshop because so much is forgotten over time. It is also important to understand that one size doesn't fit all in cybersecurity training. You need to tailor your training and approach to your audience and the varying roles in your organization. An effective program I have seen is one that periodically sends out phishing (impersonation) emails to employees. Training alone will not work. But when coupled with testing, your users are continually able to learn in a safe environment. But if you test your users without training them, they are set up for failure. Therefore, every effective user training control has two components: the training itself and ongoing testing.

Two: Privileged Access Management (PAM)

PAM encompasses both strong passwords and multi-factor authentication. Remember: it's difficult to know whether the person sitting behind the computer really is who the username and password indicate. This is because programs can be written and installed on workstations that pull user ID and password information from the endpoint's memory. Or someone can simply watch what user ID and password are used to gain access to the endpoint. When that happens, the wolf knows the user ID and password and can log in successfully. But if there is a third component added to the mix, such as a PIN that constantly changes and is sent via text message to the user's cell phone upon login, how easily can a wolf steal the expected PIN? Not easily at all.

Now that your user is authenticated, there is another way to provide an additional aspect of PAM: the least-privilege mentality. The crux here is that users should only have access to the information they need to perform their jobs. This can work on a couple of levels. First, constrain people to the data pertinent to their position. Second, allow them to access the data only when they need it. For instance, even if a user is in the payroll department, it's highly unlikely they will ever need access to that system at 2 in the morning. So you can either entirely lock out users exhibiting such behavior, or you can note it as a security incident that needs to be addressed.

In late 2014, red wolf hackers from North Korea exfiltrated Sony's emails. On the heels of that incident, Sony immediately shut down its email system and operated for two weeks without email. Can you imagine what that did to employee productivity? Although it is not known for certain, I believe that incident was the result of a hacker gaining access to a high-level administrator's credentials—which was the result of a PAM violation. Again, even the largest organizations are vulnerable to threats when controls like these are not enforced.

Three: Classification and Identification of Data

Next, when a user has been authenticated to the system, data is accessed—which is where classification and identification of data (CID) enter the equation. CID is concerned about two questions: Where is my sensitive data? Who has access to it? The first step is a data discovery process. Essentially, that process allows you to see the big picture of your sensitive data. For instance, if you want to locate where Social Security numbers are stored, you will run a discovery of your entire computing environment. And sometimes you will be surprised

> **"Even the largest organizations are vulnerable to threats when controls like these are not enforced."**

by the results. There are many instances in which your sensitive data shows up in far more places on your network than you thought they would.

Once you have located all of this data, you can decide who needs access to it. This is called access control. At this point, security solutions are available that can move sensitive data into a secure storage area on your network. These security solutions have the ability to then leave behind a stub file that gives the sensitive data's new location and the reason it was moved there. But only privileged users will have access to it. The best way to do this is to base access to data on job description and type of application used. That way, only the appropriate people will have access to sensitive information via the appropriate channels.

Four: Segregation of Data and Users

Next, segregation of data and users further defines who has access to what data. In practice, this carves up your network so that users can only access the exact data they need. Let's revisit the Target hack. Had Target segregated its point-of-sale systems from the network the HVAC company had access to, the breach never would have occurred. Thus, the type of data available on a particular network segment drives network segmentation. For instance, PCI data should never be accessible from any other network. In total, the risk posture you have decided to assume should drive segregation. When your network is properly segregated, you have a built-in insurance policy that any breach will be contained to the segment the wolves have gained access to.

Five: Incident Response

Training your organization to respond to an incident is vital to take seriously because, as the best sheepdogs know, it is not *whether* you will be breached but *when*. You must be prepared because when a breach occurs, you will have one of three responses: (1) a no incident response, (2) a well-defined incident response, or (3) an automated incident response. We will discuss these three responses at length in the next chapter. But for now, understand that you must plan for breaches.

In addition, forensics security solutions are available that also can make a significant contribution when a security event occurs. To explain how forensics security solutions work, let's imagine them like a DVR system for your TV. When a breach occurs, these security solutions enable you to go back and review the incident frame by frame. In essence, you will see every action that led to the event and every step thereafter. In fact, some of these security solutions are so feature-rich that they actually use your computer camera to take pictures of the user in front of the keyboard and monitor any user activity that occurs at that endpoint. That way, at any given moment, the security solution can show you who is sitting in front of the computer. This method of user authentication, combined with the DVR-like abilities of forensic security solutions, allows for incredible insight into security events.

John's Leadership Perspective

THE CRITICAL CONTROLS

Jim has nicely outlined five of the most critical controls that must be part of an effective cybersecurity strategy. But the majority of data breaches arise from an organization's poor understanding of its own data. When you do not understand where your data is, you will not know how to protect it. First, you must inventory your organization's data and processes. Only by having a clear picture of your internal environment can you protect every facet of it. After all, if you do not know where your sensitive data is, how can you segregate it? Moreover, how can you ensure that only certain users can access it? This point is critical because users are an organization's

> **"When you do not understand where your data is, you will not know how to protect it."**

weakest link, and that fact only compounds the damage that lack of segregation will cause.

Wolves no longer have to break passwords or use supercomputers to gain access to firewalled networks. Malware that watches a user log into systems and applications provides the wolves with everything they need to access the IT assets necessary to steal an organization's data. Today, if user credentials are compromised, so is your network. Therefore, the impact of this compromise is far greater when there is no segregation or logical boundaries of access. One of my favorite illustrations of this fact is the pilot episode of the 2004 TV series *Battlestar Galactica*. In that episode, all the ships in the fleet are interconnected by sharing a single network. When the Cylons attack, they merely have to compromise the network and upload a virus to take down the entire fleet—except for one ship that is too old to have the technology to interface with the others. That network-segregated ship is the only one that weathers the attack. If each ship had been similarly segregated, the attack would have failed.

To carry this illustration further, every user within your network should be an isolated ship with every critical domain account separated into its own flock, isolated from the rest of the sheep. We call this micro-segmentation and secure forests. By reenvisioning and reinventing the foundation of your asset protection, you can tightly control and monitor communication lines and frustrate wolves to the point that they find themselves locked in a cage. In a world where everything is connected, you need to strategically disconnect the users and networks from one another according to the logical boundaries we've discussed earlier.

As with every aspect of cybersecurity, some organizations do this poorly and some organizations do this well. To summarize, the forward-thinking organization is the one that trains its users, implements PAM, classifies and identifies its data, segregates that data and its users, and then has an incident response plan for *when* a breach occurs.

In the final chapter, we will delve deeper into three mindsets that center on incident response and allow you to identify how prepared your organization is for the security challenges that constantly surround your flock.

CHAPTER 7

REACTIVE, ACTIVE, AND ADAPTIVE ORGANIZATIONS

In my work with our clients, I see three types of organizations: reactive, active, and adaptive. The differences between each are important, as is the impact they make in the daily life of a sheepdog. When you approach security with the right mindset, you can move from constant firefighting to strategic confidence. This confidence comes from preparedness for any breach or security incident and is the prime characteristic of an adaptive organization. Whether your organization is an adaptive organization or not, this chapter aims to give you the ammunition you need to fight the wolves long before they strike. Therefore, whether you are a shepherd or a sheepdog, as you read this chapter ask yourself,

"Are we a reactive, active, or adaptive organization? And where can we do better?"

THE REACTIVE ORGANIZATION

Let's start with one of my most typical engagements: the reactive organization. Every morning, this organization's CISO buckles on his firefighter's hat at 8 a.m. and fights fires until he goes home for the night—which often doesn't happen until midnight. From an information security standpoint, this is a difficult mode in which to live. This CISO is constantly reacting to situations. It's hard to climb the ladder from there because reactive organizations typically have a budget that is too lean to reach the next level. They are not in a position to implement the right security solutions and training that could help them become what I call an active organization. But more on that later.

Organizations also remain in this mode because they reward what I call the "hero syndrome". Put simply, because this sheepdog must save the day at the last minute, he looks like a hero who swoops in just in time. This behavior is then rewarded by everything from accolades to salary increases. In reality, these CISOs are not doing the job correctly in the first place. This also dovetails with the Peter Principle that says workers tend to be promoted to their levels of incompetence.

As an example, let's consider a subpar network administrator. Instead of being fired, this network administrator is promoted because he has some knowledge of information security. The result is a bad technologist in a position in which he has no training, yet he is responsible for protecting his organization's assets. In such cases, unless I am working directly with the C-level of the organization, I can't do much to help.

I can offer products that will stop the bleeding by providing a tourniquet or a Band-Aid but, sooner or later, the hemorrhaging will start elsewhere. At its most fundamental level, this posture results from a lack of vision relating to the organization's security. There is no roadmap or blueprint to help such an organization advance. Thus, no matter how many tools such organizations have at their disposal, reactive organizations will remain the most vulnerable. The good news is this: they are not doomed to stagnate in survival mode and can move to an active posture.

But for an organization to evolve from reactive to active, it must start by changing the corporate culture and creating a vision; it must press the reset button and rebuild from the ground up. If I am working with a reactive organization, we both know it is sick. The task then becomes answering some simple questions: "How do we get better? Do we need to start by training employees? Are there security solutions that could be advantageous? And which components must be in place for an organization to realize its optimal security vision?"

> **"Thus, no matter how many tools such organizations have at their disposal, reactive organizations will remain the most vulnerable."**

I have witnessed organizations make the transition from reactive to active, so I know it is possible. In fact, one of my clients, a large regional bank, acquired a smaller bank. With that acquisition came top talent in security from the smaller bank. Through that acquisition the larger bank adopted an active risk posture because it allowed its culture to change for the better. Within a year it was not simply active but a truly adaptive organization. The first step, then, for reactive organizations to transition into becoming adaptive is to become an active organization that has the right plans, processes, and people in place to keep its assets safe.

THE ACTIVE ORGANIZATION

Active organizations focus on bettering themselves in the risk management process. They are engaged, have risk committees that meet regularly, and a C-suite and board that listen to their recommendations. They understand that risk management and mitigation don't stop after controls are implemented but must be revisited often because the threats are always changing.

But while an active organization is in a healthier position than a reactive one, it often fails to analyze its technology, its security solutions, and the data those security solutions create. This entails asking questions such as "We deployed a new security solution six months ago—how has it performed, and what has it done for us?" The organization may purchase a new security solution and integrate it into the organization's IT with adequate administrator and user training, but it is still missing a component: a structured review process. An active organization has planned reactions and business processes wrapped into security incident response, but it still finds itself slightly behind the curve adaptive organizations have set because it hasn't capitalized on the power of analysis and risk forecasting. Essentially, growth happens in a culture that continually asks, "How can we do better tomorrow than we are doing today?"

When such a mindset is in place, it takes little additional money, time, and labor to move from an active risk posture to an adaptive one (on which John will elaborate). As long as the sheepdog is willing to engage peer networks to alert the organization to threats beyond its fences and the shepherds continue to fund cybersecurity, the foundation for growth is in place. But the most vital point to understand is that if you are standing still, you are really moving backward.

The wolves are growing more cunning every day, so both sheepdog and shepherd need to work together to get ahead of them and stay there. In my experience, the best ways to do this are by bringing in a seasoned sheepdog to train a younger one, allocating budget for both security solutions and training, and incorporating analysis on the performance of said security solutions. Then an organization can become adaptive by going beyond planning its response to security incidents to automating reaction to those security incidents using the powerful security solutions at its disposal.

John's Leadership Perspective

I once worked with a leading technology organization. As I spoke with its CISO, we discussed the strength of the organization's security posture. He told me, "On a scale of zero to ten, we are a nine—maybe even a nine-and-a-half." I responded, "That is great news." But he continued, "If **"What will happen *when* we are breached?"** we ever have a breach, though, we are screwed!" That is the mindset 90 percent of companies have today—and it needs to change because it is reactive thinking.

Organizations need to think about more than their security solution sets and ask tough questions such as: "What will happen *when* we are breached? What chain of responses should be executed to address this event?" Incident management cannot simply be executed in real time. Instead, the adaptive organization manages a breach before it occurs, automating the right response.

THE ADAPTIVE ORGANIZATION

The adaptive organization displays two characteristics. The first is the strength of its commitment, and the second is its approach to cybersecurity. An adaptive organization's mentality begins with a risk-based approach, which means that it has defined its risk tolerance and identified the policies and procedures that will guide it. Cybersecurity isn't a department but a culture that permeates the organization from top to bottom. Adaptive organizations implement a core set of comprehensive controls to meet those policy statements. Then they go on the hunt, learning the wolves and analyzing them—watching their tactics and then investing in specific controls to rapidly counter their threats. Adaptive organizations no longer worry about the basics because they have confidently anticipated threats and put controls and countermeasures in place to protect against them. Most importantly, adaptive organizations place their CISOs in a position of organizational influence and allow them to influence the flock and the shepherds with equal emphasis. They don't relegate the cybersecurity role only to technology departments, but enable them to engage at all levels of the organization and business.

The adaptive organization is a mature one. It invests in its people, their partners, and their processes, and it shapes its data to be meaningful. It also understands that it cannot rely on people, processes, and controls alone; it also must implement artificial intelligence, orchestration, and automation of activities. Speed of response is the defining attribute of an adaptive organization. Its key component is its emphasis on developing automated and proactive responses to threats. At some level, it is assuming an offensive posture and putting its incident response on steroids.

To determine effectiveness, adaptive organizations focus on communication, visibility, and the awareness of the impact of a security event on its business, its customers, and its reputation. This means these organizations are asking questions such as "How are we allocating our budget? Are we still investing in security? Are we resting on our laurels and yesterday's wins? Or are we reevaluating our controls and risk tolerance on an ongoing basis? Are we engaged in risk conversations regularly? Do we have the right metrics to assess the value and effectiveness of our controls?"

In other words, they ask the right questions and continue to invest because there is no such thing as standing still. The active organization assumes a model of plan > implement > measure > reinvent. It plans for breaches, implements technology to automate the right responses, measures the effectiveness of its strategy using helpful metrics, and then it continues to invest in pushing its security capabilities ahead. It has a proactive mindset that anticipates the next breach rather than hoping that an incident will not take place.

> **"The active organization assumes a model of plan > implement > measure > reinvent."**

BECOMING AN ADAPTIVE ORGANIZATION

Whether you are a reactive or active organization today, realize that you will not become an adaptive organization overnight. But you can become one. Start by developing a vision for your security. You need a strategy and a roadmap to plot your course. Begin by summarizing all of your risk and identifying the key controls you will need to implement by using a risk-based approach to actualize the security posture and risk profile your organization desires.

Once you have accomplished all that, you can tailor your strategy and implementation to specific threats and their nuances. By employing advanced threat intelligence coupled with automation and quasi-artificial intelligence analytical workflows, you will be able to build a cyber capability that can detect threats early, frustrate the wolf, automate response and recovery, and keep the precious assets of your organization—the sheep—safe. And this, of course, is the goal of every sheepdog.

So where is your organization today? Are you reactive, active, or adaptive? If you're reactive, where do you need to invest to improve? If you're active, what are the small—*yet significant*—changes you need to make? What would these changes cost the organization, and is the budget available to realize them? When you have the right plan in place and become an adaptive organization, it's time to go on the offensive. You will be able to focus on what's ahead rather than what's on fire now. Your sheepdog will be alert and well equipped to do the job right. And when that happens, let the wolf hunt begin.

CONCLUSION

Our goal in writing this book is to help you take the first steps toward becoming an adaptive organization. We want to equip shepherd and sheepdog alike to protect their flock from the visible and invisible threats trying to breach the fences every day. So where is your organization, and how safe is your data? What would happen if you were breached tomorrow? Do you have automated responses in place, or will that be another fire to fight?

No matter where you are today, the first step is a desire to improve. Strive to be an organization of excellence rather than one driven only by compliance. Consistently measure and assess your people, processes, and controls to determine both your strengths and weaknesses. But if you are a shepherd without a battle-hardened sheepdog, then make the decision to hire one—whether that means promoting the right person from within or bringing one in from the outside. Nevertheless, just as in our opening story, shepherds cannot tend to every aspect of their sheep alone. Nor can they keep vigil over the pasture's entire perimeter.

But with the right sheepdog at your side, you will be ready for the wolves even before they breach your perimeter. Adaptive organizations are those that survive breaches because they stop wolves dead in their tracks before they can escape with their sheep. Adaptive organizations will nurture and protect the strongest flocks and maintain their most valuable assets into the indefinite future because they hear the warning calls from the sheepdogs just over the hill. Yes, the wolves are cunning, their motives are sinister, and their methods vary. But the right sheepdogs have DNA hard-wired to preempt and guard against attacks at every layer. The best sheepdogs allow the shepherd to sleep soundly at night because they know exactly how to remain ever-vigilant against enemies that never rest.

ABOUT THE AUTHORS

Jim Shaeffer

 Born in San Antonio, TX, Jim moved at an early age to Alaska and grew up in South Dakota—instilling in him a great love of the outdoors. His grandfather and father spent many enjoyable hours with young Jim teaching him to love everything in nature. Entering the workforce after having taken every college computer course offered at South Dakota State University and Augustana College, Jim began his IT career as a programmer at Raven Industries in Sioux Falls, SD. He then joined UES/Spectrum where he spent most of his time traveling throughout

the United States, installing Texas Instruments mini-computers at post-secondary, proprietary educational institutions. Booth Newspapers, a chain of eight news-papers located in Michigan outside of Detroit, hired Jim as a systems analyst when he was only twenty five. Jim relocated to Michigan for the next twenty seven years. After five years with Booth, Jim became the IT Director at Symplex Communications in Ann Arbor, MI, where he worked for three years. He then founded JCS & Associates, Inc. in 1991 and he continues to serve as its CEO. Jim now lives in South Dakota and enjoys spending time in the outdoors and traveling to Michigan to spend time with his grown children.

John Paul Cunningham

John Paul Cunningham is a technology executive with deep expertise in technology governance, risk management, and information security.

He brings twenty three years of experience delivering mission-critical solutions to Fortune 50 companies in the financial services and manufacturing sectors and twenty eight years of experience overall delivering technology, risk, and security solutions.

A visionary in anticipating technology trends and innovation, he maintains a pragmatic, solution-oriented approach and excels in tailoring technology to best address the needs of the enterprise in developing and executing strategies that protect the organization from cyber threats.

His ability to translate complex technical issues into plain, understandable language enables him to collaborate effectively across the organization and with customers, external auditors, and regulators alike while leading the technical teams responsible for ongoing development and delivery of global services.

John has led Financial Services Peer Advisory forums of chief information security officers and has been a featured panelist on several industry-wide financial technology forums and conferences. He is a retired federal (DOD) qualified law enforcement officer and a veteran of the Gulf War in Iraq and Kuwait. In addition, he holds both the CISSP and PMP professional certifications as well as a variety of technical security certifications.

ABOUT THE COMPANY

JCS & Associates, Inc.

After fourteen years of employment in various IT capacities, Jim Shaeffer decided to start his own business as a computer consultant, specializing in IT security. In February of 1991, he formed JCS & Associates, Inc. as a security consulting organization. During the first year of business, Jim realized that his consultative approach to serving his customers led to the sales of many IT security solutions to those customers. He then began using his consulting skills to provide a "consultative sales approach" that led to immediate success in selling IT security solutions to organizations of all sizes. JCS & Associates, Inc. has grown in size and scope and now specializes in IT security assessments and the sale of complementary IT security solutions to businesses and organizations of all sizes. Using its proven consultative sales approach in combination with security assessments of its prospects' environments, JCS & Associates, Inc. provides the knowledge gained through the security assessment process to implement custom-tailored solutions and successfully integrates those solutions into its customer's environment. But it doesn't stop there—the JCS team regularly provides "after the sale" support to its customers. That support results in satisfied customers who stay with the JCS-provided IT security solutions and purchase other complementary IT security solutions from the JCS team.

Please contact us at:
JCS & Associates, Inc.
800-968-9527
info@jcsaainc.com
www.jcsaainc.com